Contents

Tell me about...

Running

▲ Dawn Harper of the United States in lane 6 crosses the line first to win a gold medal at the 2008 Olympic Games in Beijing, China.

People have held running races for thousands of years. At the very first Ancient Olympics, held over 2,700 years ago, there was only one event: a 190-metre running race called a *stade*. The race gave its name to the word stadium.

Runners compete in races over different distances. The shortest events, over 60m, 100m and 200m, are known as sprints. Events such as the 800m and 1500m are called middle distance races. The 5,000m and 10,000m races and the marathon are long distance events.

Today, millions of people run for exercise and fitness. Over 34,000 people, for instance, finished the 2008 London Marathon. Some like to race against others, pushing themselves to run the fastest that they can.

The very fastest runners in the world are record-breaking athletes. At the 2008 Olympics, Usain Bolt from Jamaica ran the 100m in just 9.69 seconds, setting a new world record.

You may not break a world record, but you can achieve a personal best. This is when you run your fastest ever time for a distance. Whether you win a race or not, beating your own best time should make you very proud. It's something that top professional athletes aim to do too.

▼ Running races may be against others but really, running is a test of your own speed and ability.

Finishing first

Nothing beats the feeling of crossing the finishing line first in a race. Behind the glory of winning, though, there is a combination of skill and hard work.

▼ It is an amazing thrill to win a race and receive a trophy, medal or certificate. It will spur on many athletes to train even harder.

▼ The runner in lane 4 is close to winning the race. She will thrust her chest forward as she runs through the finishing line.

To learn to run well, you need to work with an athletics coach or teacher. Coaches can give you exercises called drills to improve your fitness, speed and running technique. That includes how you finish a race.

Towards the end of a race, you may start to feel tired. You might find it more of a struggle to run smoothly and, chances are, you

▲ Gail Devers of the USA and Merlene Ottey of Jamaica finish with the exact same time at the 1993 World Championship 100m final. Officials decided that Devers won the gold medal.

will start to slow down. Top runners train really hard so they can fight this tiredness, which is known as fatigue. They try to stay relaxed and balanced throughout the whole race.

You must try to keep running as you cross the finishing line. This is because you only complete a race when your body crosses the line, not your arms or your legs. Young runners sometimes lose races if they do not time their finish well or slow down as they reach the line.

Really close finishes in major competitions are judged by high speed photographs. These can separate out who has won, even if two runners record exactly the same time.

Photo finishes

At the 2007 World Championships, Lauryn Williams and Veronica Campbell finished the 100m with the same time – 11.01 seconds. Photo finishes showed that Campbell had won...just!

At the 2002 European Championships, Mehdi Baala and Reyes Estevez ran the 1500m race and crossed the line together. A photo finish showed Baala had won by just two thousandths of a second.

The track and kit

You will do most of your running on an athletics track. At school, this may be marked out on grass. In stadiums, tracks are made of a special surface which provides grip. Outdoor tracks are 400m long. Different races have different starting points. These are marked out on the track.

Tracks are usually marked out with eight lanes. Lane 1 is the lane closest to the inside and lane 8, the furthest. Runners in the 100m, 200m and 400m have to stay in their lane, otherwise they will be disqualified. This means they cannot take part in the race.

In longer races, runners may start in a lane but, after a certain distance, they can break. This means they can leave their lane. Runners usually move to the inside lane as this is the shortest distance around the track.

▼ Runners in a 200m race start from different positions. This is called a staggered start. It makes sure that all the runners run the same distance to the finish.

▲ Running fast around a bend in the 200m can force you out of your lane if you are not balanced. The runner in lane 2 has stepped on the inside lane next to his. He will be disqualified.

When a runner completes the full length of the track, this is called a lap. In longer races, you may have to run many laps of the track. Runners try to run at an even pace for most of the race.

When you are starting out you need a running vest or t-shirt, shorts and good trainers. Top track runners wear shoes with short spikes in the sole for grip. A tracksuit is also important as it will help you to keep warm between races.

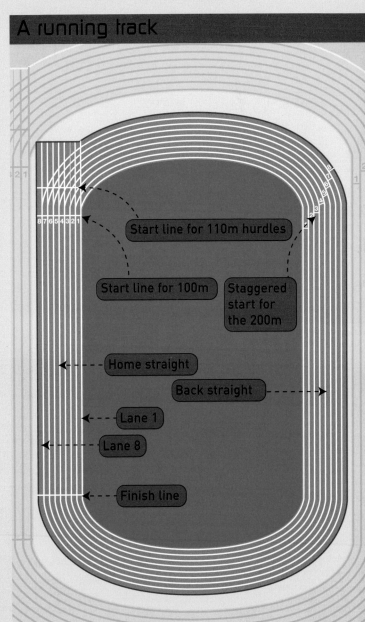

A running track

Start line for 110m hurdles

Start line for 100m

Staggered start for the 200m

Home straight

Back straight

Lane 1

Lane 8

Finish line

Star runners

Top runners take part in races all over the world. The world's best runners become famous. Some become rich too, as many competitions offer prize money to the winners and pay the runners a fee for appearing.

▼ British hurdler Stu Jackson stretches some of his leg muscles before training. Stretching helps prevent injuries and helps your muscles work at their best.

Runners spend hundreds of hours in training. They work very closely with their coach and follow a strict diet. Runners not only have to be able to run fast. They also need

▲ Usain Bolt of Jamaica poses next to the Beijing Olympic stadium's electronic timer which shows his 100m world record of just 9.69 seconds.

strength. Sprinters especially need great power to surge forward at the start of their race.

Sadly, some professional runners have tried to cheat by taking drugs. Some drugs can improve athletes' performance by letting them build muscle quickly or train harder for longer periods. Athletes found guilty of taking drugs can be banned from entering competitions for two years or for life.

Amazing athletes

As a child, Wilma Rudolph suffered from the disease polio. She could only walk with leg braces. Yet she trained very hard, and in 1960 won the 100m, 200m and 4 x 100m relay races at the Olympics.

In 1968, Kenyan runner Kip Keino got caught in a traffic jam before his 1500m race. He had to jog more than 1.6km to the Olympic stadium yet still won the race and gold medal.

Josiah Thugwane was mugged and shot in South Africa. Yet he recovered to win the marathon at the 1996 Olympics just five months later.

Sprints

Sprints are probably the most exciting of running events. Millions tune in to watch male and female sprinters compete in thrilling races over 60m, 100m and 200m.

A sprint race begins with the starter calling, "On your marks". You place your hands just behind the starting line.

On the call of "Set", you raise your hips up and press your feet hard against the track, ready to race.

▲ Experienced sprinters use starting blocks to begin their races. These are metal bars with large wedges fitted to them.

▼ At the start of a sprint race, you should be in a low position during your first few steps. Then you need to straighten and run upright.

When the starter fires a gun or shouts "Go!", you drive hard against the track, pushing yourself forward. Your back leg travels forward to take your first step, called a stride.

You need to start as fast as possible, but you should try to avoid making a false start. This is where the officials judge you have left your starting block before the starter's gun.

New rules in professional athletics mean that, after one false start has occurred, the next person to make a false start will be disqualified. Electronic sensors fitted to the starting blocks work out if a sprinter has made a false start.

▼ This photo shows the men's 200m final at the 2008 Olympics. Sprinters run with a good rhythm, looking straight ahead. They pump their arms backwards and forwards to help keep their speed.

Middle distance running

The main middle distance events are the 800m and 1500m. In the 800m, runners start in lanes just as for sprint races. After the first bend (at about 100m), they can break (see page 10), and head towards the inside lane. In the 1500m, runners start along the same line and can move immediately to the inside lane if they want to.

▼ Runners stand up and lean forward for the start of a 1500m race. They wait for the starter's gun to begin the race.

When you are taking part in a middle distance race, it is usually impossible to run flat out for the whole distance. Some runners get over-excited and run too fast at the start. This leaves them too tired to compete at the finish. It's important to judge carefully how fast you run during the different stages of the race.

Try to run smoothly with your body upright and your shoulders level. Your arms should swing back and forth, but not as fiercely as when you are sprinting.

A bell rings to signal the last lap of a middle and long distance race. Then the pressure builds as runners try to get to the front or into position to challenge the leader. As you come round the final bend you will be tired, but you must try to sprint as hard as you can to reach the finish.

▼ To run middle distance races well, try to run on the balls of your feet with a bouncy stride. As you push off your back leg, it should straighten behind you.

Hurdling

The base points towards runners.

▲ Hurdles have to be the correct height for your age. Your coach will adjust the hurdles to the right height for you.

▼ You push off your back leg and lift your front leg high at the knee. Straighten your front leg to get it over the hurdle. Pull up your back leg and turn your foot outwards. Bring your back leg round and forward to land on the track.

Hurdling races are a great test of speed and skill. Top hurdlers complete 100m and 400m races in only a few seconds more than runners who are racing without having to jump over hurdles.

There are ten hurdles to clear in the women's 100m and men's 110m. Hurdles have a base which means that they will fall over if they are knocked during a race. Runners are allowed to knock over hurdles in the race but it will slow them down and sometimes make them fall.

The base of the hurdle always points towards the runner. Never try to jump a hurdle from the wrong side. You can hurt yourself really badly if you do.

Good hurdling technique feels strange at first and you will need lots of practice to master it. You raise your front leg and thrust it over the hurdle. You turn your back leg outwards and pull it up and over the hurdle.

Top hurdlers need to be very flexible. They do a lot of muscle-stretching exercises. They also work with their coaches on their stride pattern. This is the number of steps they take in between hurdles.

Top hurdlers

American Ed Moses set a record when he won 122 400m hurdle races in a row between 1977 and 1987.

Liu Xiang won the 110m hurdles at the 2004 Olympics. It was China's first ever running gold medal. Two years later Xiang broke the world record with a time of 12.88 seconds.

▼ China's Liu Xiang leads at the 2004 Olympics 110m hurdles final. A top level hurdles race is an amazing sight. The hurdlers barely seem to alter their running style as they sprint down the straight.

Relay racing

Relay races may be fun events at school, but they are very important in professional athletics. The relays are often the final races at major competitions like the Olympics.

There are two main relay races in major athletics. Both feature four runners who all run the same distance. The 4 x 400m is one lap of the track per runner. You pass on a hollow tube called a baton to the next runner who stands on the track finish line.

The 4 x 100m is the most dramatic relay event. You sprint as hard as you can to complete your 100m of the race with

▼ The baton can be swept up or swept down into the receiver's hand. When receivers feel the baton in their grasp, they close their hand to grip it and sprint away.

World records

Men
4 x 100m 37.10 seconds – Jamaica, 2008
4 x 400m 2 minutes, 54.29 seconds – USA, 1993

Women
4 x 100m 41.37 seconds –
East Germany, 1985
4 x 400m 3 minutes, 15.17 seconds –
USSR, 1988

Start of the changeover zone

▲ The receiver starts sprinting a few metres before the start of the changeover zone.

the baton in one hand. As you near your team-mate, he or she starts to sprint.

You need to time the passing of the baton well. It must take place inside a marked-out part of the track which is 20m long. This is called the changeover zone. Runners train hard to make sure that they pass the baton really smoothly to each other.

Relay teams think hard about the order in which they will all run. Often, a team will put their fastest runner in the last leg of a relay. But all runners must do their best if the team is to have a chance of winning.

Dropped baton

▲ Relay runners need to communicate well. You can lose time with a slow baton change or if you drop a baton.

End of the changeover zone

▲ If a runner steps out of the changeover zone before the baton is in the receiver's hand, then the whole team is disqualified.

Long distance running

▲ Male athletes running the 2008 Olympic marathon. It was won by Kenya's Samuel Kamau Wansiru in 2 hours, 6 minutes and 32 seconds, a new Olympic record.

Long distance races are run over distances of 3,000m right up to the 42.2km-long marathon. Top long distance runners need good speed and strength. They also need stamina. This is the ability to run really well for long periods of time.

Racing in long distance events involves running lap after lap of a normal 400m track. In the case of the 10,000m, that's 25 laps! Yet the top runners like Ethiopia's Haile Gebrselassie can still sprint the last 100-200m of a race. The other main events run on a regular track are the 5,000m and 3,000m.

The 3,000m steeplechase is an unusual event. Runners have to jump or hurdle large barriers 28 times in a race. They also have to clear a water jump seven times.

Some long distance running is carried out over cross-country courses, through woods, up hills and down into valleys. Other events, such as the marathon, are held over courses through city streets.

The marathon is the ultimate long distance running test. Top athletes now complete the course in less than two and a quarter hours. A marathon usually ends with a single lap of an athletics track.

Marathon magic

The world's fastest marathon was run in 2 hours 4 minutes and 26 seconds by Haile Gebrselassie in 2007. The great Ethiopian was also unbeaten at 10,000m from 1993 to 2001!

Another Ethiopian, Abebe Bikila, won the 1960 Olympic marathon. He ran the race in bare feet.

The Czech long distance runner Emil Zatopek won the 5,000m, the 10,000m and the marathon at the same Olympics in 1952.

▼ Runners in a steeplechase have the choice of hurdling obstacles or, if they are tired, they can put their foot on the top of the barrier and jump off it.

Running tactics

Most runners aim to run at a fast, even speed for all, or nearly all, of a race. With longer races, it is possible to change how you race. Trying different ways of racing is called using tactics. Runners change their tactics based on their own strengths and weaknesses. They also have to think about the conditions (for example, whether it is raining or windy) and the competitors they are racing against.

Some runners prefer to go faster at the start to get ahead and then try to stretch their lead. This is called running from the front and it can be very hard and tiring.

Other runners choose to stay in the pack with most of the other runners. Near the end of the race, they increase their speed and hope to sprint past their rivals. In a close race when all the runners

▲ Long and middle distance running is tiring especially if you are running from the front. Sometimes, when a group of runners breaks away from the others, the athletes in the group will take turns to run at the front. They aim to keep lots of distance between them and the runners behind them.

▲ When you are running a middle distance race, stay aware of your position among the other runners. You do not want to be boxed in with only a short distance of the race still to go.

are bunched together, athletes have to be careful. They have to avoid becoming boxed in, or trapped by other runners so that they cannot get near the front.

Tactics can change from one race to the next. At top competitions, many runners have to take part in races called heats or rounds. The best runners from these races go into the semi-finals or final race. Some runners choose to slow down to save energy for a later race. Others prefer to run flat out and record a fast time to make their rivals nervous.

Drastic tactics

Before there were digital watches, Paavo Nurmi used to race with a stopwatch in his hand. It did not stop him winning an amazing nine Olympic gold medals!

Kenyan John Kagwe had to stop twice to do up his shoe laces during the 1997 New York City Marathon. He still won!

▼ If you have a sprint finish, you need to time it well. The runner on the left has been running behind the leader. When he is ready to overtake, he moves out onto the shoulder of the leader before running past him.

The world of running

Running races range from competitions between local schools right up to international championships. Most countries have their own national athletics competition. These events can be important as the best runners may qualify to represent their country at a major international competition.

▼ American 400m star Jeremy Wariner (holding the baton) leads the 4x400m relay at the 2008 Olympics.

In the winter, indoor competitions are popular. For many top runners, indoor racing helps them prepare for the outdoor season in the spring and summer. Indoor races take place on a 200m track. The 100m sprint is replaced by a 60m sprint and the 100m and 110m hurdles are replaced by the 60m hurdles.

Outdoors, runners compete in major events held mostly in Europe and at continental championships such as the Pan-American games. The biggest competitions include the World Athletics Championships which is now held every two years.

The Summer Olympics is the biggest competition of all. Held every four years, top runners dedicate much of their lives to try and win its biggest prize, an Olympic gold medal. Millions of people tune in to watch the top runners compete in the Olympics.

Record wins

At the 1948 Olympics, Fanny Blankers-Koen from the Netherlands set a record by winning four gold medals at the same games.

Usain Bolt won the 100m and 200m at the 2008 Olympics, breaking the world record time for each event.

▶
Maria Mutola of Mozambique wins her 800m race at the 2006 World Indoor Championships.

27

Where next?

These websites and books will help you to find out more about running.

Websites

http://www.kidsrunning.com/

Produced by *Runner's World*, this is one of the best running websites for children.

http://www.justrun.org

There's lots of advice on diet, training and running tips at this useful website.

http://news.bbc.co.uk/sport1/hi/athletics/skills

Watch videos, animations and read tips about how to perform well from the BBC. Check out the 'Get Involved' section of the website as well.

http://www.olympic.org/uk

Learn about all the running events at the Olympics including past champions from Athens in 1896 to Beijing in 2008.

http://www.iaaf.org

Read news and see action from important meetings at the website of the IAAF, the organisation that runs world athletics.

Books

Track Events in Action by John Crossingham and Bobbie Kalman (Crabtree Publishing, Canada, 2004)
Information about all the different running races.

A World-class Sprinter by Clive Gifford (Heinemann Library, 2005)
A description of how sprinting champions train and compete.

Running words

back straight the straight part of the track furthest away from the finishing line

baton the short tube passed between relay runners in a race

changeover zone a marked out area of the track where the baton is passed between runners in a relay race

disqualified barred from competing in an event for having broken a rule of the race

false start an error made by an athlete when he or she moves forward before the start of the race

heat an early race in an event with the best runners advancing to a final or semi-final

pack the main group of runners in a middle and long distance race

personal best (PB) your best ever time for a particular event

stride pattern the number of steps a hurdler takes between hurdles

warming up carrying out a series of exercises before a race to get your mind and body ready to compete

Index

Numbers in **bold** refer to pictures.